Markets

This is a market

and this is a market too.

A market can have carts and vans.

A market can be on boats!

A market can be in a park.

Markets can be
in the dark.

This night market is
in Hong Kong.

You can shop for lots of
things at a market.

You can shop for
carpets and hats...

…dishes and bags.

You can get yarn and art!

Food is a big thing at markets too.

There is farm food
at the market.

You can get jars of
jam and tarts.

You can get sweets and nuts and hotdogs! Yum!

It is fun to visit a market.

Words to blend

boats	**night**	**Hong Kong**
this	**things**	**yum**
shop	**food**	**sweets**
dishes	**vans**	**fun**
lots	**hats**	**bags**
jam	**nuts**	**visit**
market	**hotdogs**	**farms**

Before reading

Synopsis: This text looks at all the different things found at markets all over the world.

Review graphemes/phonemes: th/th, ng/nk, sh, ee, igh, oa, oo/oo

New grapheme/phoneme: ar

Book discussion: Look at the cover and read the title together. Ask: *Have you ever been shopping in a market? What was it like? What kinds of things could you buy there?*

Link to prior learning: Display the grapheme ar. Say: *These two letters are a digraph. They make one sound.* Write or display these words: *market, park, garden, farm.* How quickly can children identify the *ar* grapheme and read the words?

Vocabulary check: yarn – thread that is used in knitting or sewing

Decoding practice: Turn to pages 14–15. How quickly can children find and read two words with *ar*? (*jars, tarts*)

Tricky word practice: Display the word was and ask children to circle the tricky part of the word (*a*, which makes an /o/ sound). Practise writing and reading this word.

After reading

Apply learning: Ask: *Which market in the book did you think was most unusual or interesting? Why?*

Comprehension

- Where was the night market?

- Are all markets the same?

- What would you like to buy from a market? Choose something you can see in the book.

Fluency

- Pick a page that most of the group read quite easily. Ask them to reread it with pace and expression. Model how to do this if necessary.

- Ask children to choose a page they found interesting, and read it aloud with appropriate pace and expression.

- Practise reading the words on page 17.

Tricky words review

and	have	be
the	you	for
of	was	to
there	too	in
at	it	a